Introduction

Quilters sometimes have a dilemma. It's nice to add quilting touches that can be changed with the seasons throughout the house, but we're often short on time. How do we decorate for the different times of the year without spending a lot of time making projects? The answer is to make small projects.

We asked our designers to come up with small seasonal projects, and what they sent us fits the bill perfectly. From pillows to table runners to wall quilts to small throws, this book is full of projects that will add decorative quilted touches throughout the year. And, if you need a quick gift, we've got you covered. These projects are suitable for gift-giving as well! Pull up a seat and start browsing these pages. Your next design is just waiting for you to start.

Table of Contents

T0340733

Patchwork Heart Table Runner

Make a statement with big, bold hearts in this fun and modern table runner full of love.

Design by Michelle Freedman
Quilted by Chris Batten

Skill Level
Confident Beginner

Finished Sizes
Runner Size: 54" x 18"
Block Size: 18" x 18"
Number of Blocks: 3

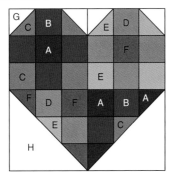

Heart
18" x 18" Finished Block
Make 3

Materials
- ⅓ yard dark red*
- ⅝ yard medium red*
- ⅓ yard light red*
- ⅓ yard coral*
- ⅓ yard light coral*
- ⅓ yard dark coral*
- ⅞ yard white*
- 1¼ yards backing fabric
- 22" x 58" batting
- Thread
- Basic sewing tools and supplies

Fabrics from Shadow Play collection from Maywood Studio used to make sample.

Project Notes
Read all instructions before beginning this project.

Stitch right sides together using a ¼" seam allowance unless otherwise specified.

Materials and cutting lists assume 40" of usable fabric width for yardage.

Arrows indicate directions to press seams.

WOF – width of fabric
HST – half-square triangle �
QST – quarter-square triangle ⊠

Cutting

From dark red cut:
- 12 (3½") A squares

From medium red cut:
- 18 (3½") B squares
- 4 (2½" x WOF) binding strips

From light red cut:
- 15 (3½") C squares

From coral cut:
- 18 (3½") D squares

From light coral cut:
- 15 (3½") E squares

From dark coral cut:
- 12 (3½") F squares

From white cut:
- 12 (3½") G squares
- 6 (9½") H squares

Here's a Tip

Make it a mini—cut the squares at 2½" or even 1½" and create a smaller version of the original.

Inspiration

"My inspiration for this quilt was to use a traditional patchwork technique—in this case, a nine-patch—within the shape of a big heart. The idea was to use a set of four nine-patch units for each block to create a scrappy/random feel. By organizing the blocks this way, the heart shapes stitch together quickly." —Michelle Freedman

Completing the Blocks

1. Refer to Sew & Flip Corners on page 8 and use six of each C and G squares to make six C-G HST units (Figure 1).

C-G HST
Make 6

Figure 1

E-G HST
Make 6

Figure 2

2. In the same manner, use six of each E and G squares to make six E-G HST units (Figure 2).

3. Arrange two C-G HST units, two C squares, four B squares and one A square in three rows as shown (Figure 3). Sew units and squares together in rows; join the rows to make one unit 1. Make three.

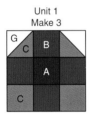

Unit 1
Make 3

Figure 3

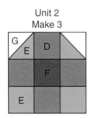

Unit 2
Make 3

Figure 4

4. In the same manner, make one unit 2 using two E-G HST units, two E squares, four D squares and one F square (Figure 4). Make three.

5. Arrange and sew together three F squares, two D squares and one E square as shown (Figure 5a). Make three.

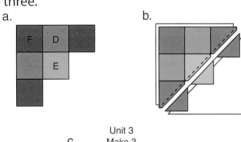

a.   b.

c.

Unit 3
Make 3

Figure 5

6. Referring again to Sew & Flip Corners, place a step 5 unit and an H square right sides together,

aligning the corners (Figure 5b). With the wrong side of the step 5 unit facing up, draw a stitching line corner to corner, intersecting the seam lines of the step 5 unit. Stitch, trim and press open to make one unit 3 (Figure 5c). Make three.

Here's a Tip

Use spray starch or sizing to help control stretching along the diagonal edges.

7. In the same manner, use three A squares, two B squares, one C square and one H square to make one unit 4 (Figure 6). Make three.

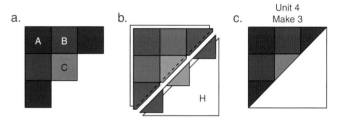

a.   b.   c.

Unit 4
Make 3

Figure 6

8. Refer to the Heart block diagram and arrange one of each unit 1–4 in two rows. Sew the units together in rows; join the rows to complete the block. Make three.

Completing the Runner

1. Refer to the Assembly Diagram and arrange the three blocks together in one row, reversing the direction of the center block.

2. Sew the blocks together to complete the runner top.

3. Layer, baste, quilt as desired and bind referring to Quilting Basics. The photographed runner was quilted with an edge-to-edge geometric texture. ●

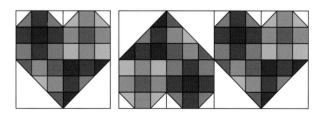

Heart Table Runner
Assembly Diagram 54" x 18"

Sunrise in Spring

The modified Hunter's Star block used in this design ushers in spring with its breezy pinwheels.

Designed & Quilted by Annette Falvo

Skill Level

Intermediate

Finished Sizes

Table Topper Size: 40" x 40"

Block Size: 10" x 10"

Number of Blocks: 16

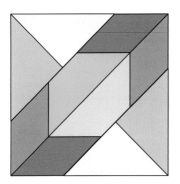

Sunrise
10" x 10" Finished Block
Make 16

Materials

- ⅞ yard medium orange tonal*
- ⅞ yard medium pink tonal*
- ½ yard light blue tonal*
- ½ yard light green tonal*
- ⅝ yard light blue print*
- ⅝ yard light green print*
- ½ yard light green binding fabric*
- 2¾ yards backing*
- 44" x 44" batting
- Basic sewing tools and supplies

*Fabrics from the Happy Hearts and Shadow Blush collections from Benartex used to make sample.

Project Notes

Read all instructions before beginning this project.

Refer to Cutting Diagrams to cut A and B patches. Yardage amounts assume patches are cut nested.

Stitch right sides together using a ¼" seam allowance unless otherwise specified.

Materials and cutting lists assume 40" of usable fabric width for yardage.

Arrows indicate directions to press seams.

WOF – width of fabric

HST – half-square triangle ◻

QST – quarter-square triangle ⊠

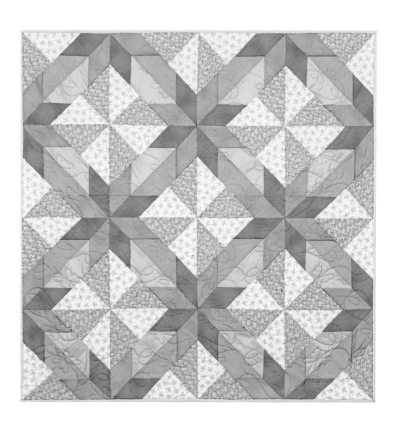

Inspiration

"Springtime's sunny mornings and breezy afternoons inspired me to create a fresh, colorful table topper." —Annette Falvo

Cutting

From each medium orange tonal and medium pink tonal cut:

- 4 (2⅞" x WOF) strips. Subcut into 32 A diamonds.

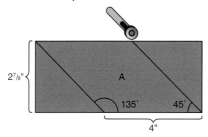

Cutting Diagram 1

From each light blue tonal and light green tonal cut:

- 4 (2⅞" x WOF) strips. Subcut into 16 B trapezoids.

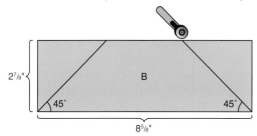

Cutting Diagram 2

Here's a Tip

The A and B patches are cut on the bias, which means they can easily be distorted due to stretching. To help stabilize the fabric, press the fabric strips with a good amount of starch before cutting them. Handle the patches carefully and "press" with an up and down motion rather than "ironing" with a sideways motion.

From each light blue print and light green print cut:

- 8 (7⅞") squares, then cut twice diagonally ⊠ to make 32 C QSTs

From light green binding fabric cut:

- 5 (2½" x WOF) binding strips

Completing the Blocks

1. Lay out one orange A diamond, one blue B trapezoid and one pink A diamond. Join to make one blue A-B-A unit (Figure 1). Make 16.

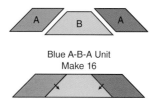

Figure 1

2. In the same way and noting placement of the pink and orange A diamonds, use a green B trapezoid to make one green A-B-A unit (Figure 2). Make 16.

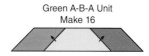

Figure 2

3. Join one blue A-B-A unit and one green A-B-A unit to make a center section (Figure 3). Make 16.

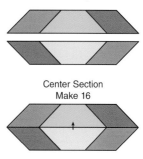

Figure 3

4. Join short edges of one blue print C QST and one green print C QST to make a corner section (Figure 4). Make 32.

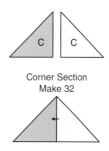

Figure 4

5. Lay out two corner sections and one center section (Figure 5). Join as shown to complete one Sunrise block. Make 16.

Block
Make 16

Figure 5

Completing the Table Topper

1. Referring to the Assembly Diagram, lay out the blocks in four rows of four blocks each, noting the orientation of the blocks.

2. Sew the blocks into rows and join the rows to complete the table topper. Press.

3. Layer, baste, quilt as desired and bind referring to Quilting Basics. The photographed table topper was quilted with a butterfly and loop design. ●

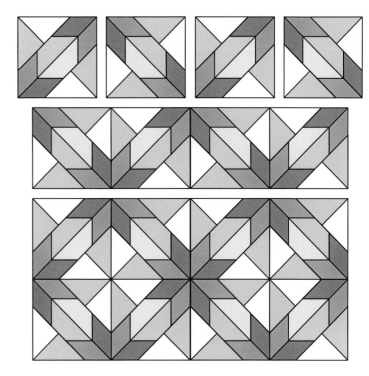

Sunrise in Spring
Assembly Diagram 40" x 40"

SEW & FLIP CORNERS

Use this method to add triangle corners in a quilt block.

1. Draw a diagonal line from corner to corner on the wrong side of the specified square. Place the square, right sides together, on the indicated corner of the larger piece, making sure the line is oriented in the correct direction indicated by the pattern (Figure 1).

2. Sew on the drawn line. Trim ¼" away from sewn line (Figure 2).

Figure 1   **Figure 2**

3. Open and press to reveal the corner triangle (Figure 3).

Figure 3

4. If desired, square up the finished unit to the required unfinished size. ●

In a Row

Quick flower blocks are a lovely addition to a spring table!

Design by Wendy Sheppard
Quilted by Darlene Szabo of Sew Graceful Quilting

Skill Level
Confident Beginner

Finished Sizes
Runner Size: 49½" x 17"
Block Size: 7½" x 11"
Number of Blocks: 5

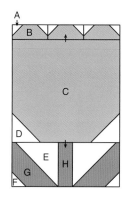

Flower
7½" x 11" Finished Block
Make 5

Materials
- ¾ yard background*
- ¼ yard each yellow, aqua and red prints*
- ⅛ yard light green print*
- ½ yard green dot*
- ¾ yard backing*
- 21" x 53" batting*
- Thread*
- Basic sewing tools and supplies

Fabrics from the 30s Playtime collection by Chloe's Closet for Moda Fabrics; 50 wt. Mako thread from Aurifil; Tuscany silk batting from Hobbs Bonded Fibers used to make sample. EQ8 was used to design this quilt.

Project Notes
Read all instructions before beginning this project.

Stitch right sides together using a ¼" seam allowance unless otherwise specified.

Materials and cutting lists assume 40" of usable fabric width for yardage.

Arrows indicate directions to press seams.

WOF – width of fabric
HST – half-square triangle ◻
QST – quarter-square triangle ⊠

Cutting

From background cut:
- 10 (3½") E squares
- 2 (2½" x 13½") K rectangles
- 4 (2½" x 11½") I rectangles
- 10 (2½") D squares
- 3 (2½" x WOF) strips, stitch short ends to short ends, then subcut into:
     2 (2½" x 50") L strips
- 2 (1½" x WOF) strips, stitch short ends to short ends, then subcut into:
     1 (1½" x 46") J strip
     10 (1½") F squares
- 30 (1¼") A squares

From each yellow and aqua print cut:
- 2 (7½" x 8") C rectangles (4 total)
- 6 (1½" x 3") B rectangles (12 total)

From red print cut:
- 1 (7½" x 8") C rectangle
- 3 (1½" x 3") B rectangles

From light green print cut:

- 2 (1½" x WOF) strips, stitch short ends to short ends, then subcut into:
    - 1 (1½" x 46") J strip

From green dot cut:

- 10 (3½" x 3¾") G rectangles
- 3 (1½" x 3½") H rectangles
- 4 (2½" x WOF) binding strips

Completing the Blocks

1. Refer to Sew & Flip Corners on page 8 and sew A squares to the top corners of the B rectangles to make 15 A-B units (Figure 1).

A-B Unit
Make 15

Make 5

Figure 1   **Figure 2**

2. Join three matching A-B units together along the short edges as shown (Figure 2). Make five.

3. Refer again to Sew & Flip Corners and sew D squares to the bottom corners of the C rectangles, along the long edge (Figure 3). Make five.

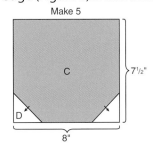

Make 5

7½"

8"

Figure 3

4. In the same manner, with the long sides of a G rectangle at the top and bottom, sew an E square to the upper right corner and an F square to the bottom left corner (Figure 4a). Repeat to make a mirror-image unit (Figure 4b). Make five of each.

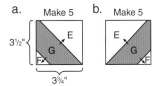

a. Make 5   b. Make 5

3½"

3¾"

Figure 4

5. Sew mirror-image step 4 units to opposite sides of an H rectangle to make a leaf unit (Figure 5). Make five.

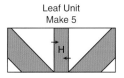

Leaf Unit
Make 5

H

Figure 5

6. Refer to the Flower block diagram and sew together matching units from steps 2 and 3; join to a leaf unit to complete one block. Make five.

Completing the Runner

1. Refer to the Assembly Diagram and sew together blocks alternating with I rectangles to make the block row.

2. Sew the background J strip to the top and the light green J strip to the bottom of the block row.

3. Sew the K rectangles to the short ends; sew the L strips to opposite long sides to complete the runner top.

4. Layer, baste, quilt as desired and bind to finish, referring to Quilting Basics. The photographed runner was quilted with allover swirls and flowers. ●

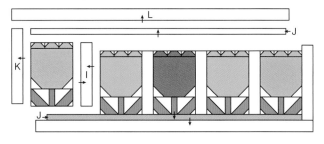

L

J

K

I

J

In a Row
Assembly Diagram 49½" x 17"

American Pride

You can almost hear a marching band when you see this stirring display of red, white and blue!

Designed & Quilted by Joy Heimark

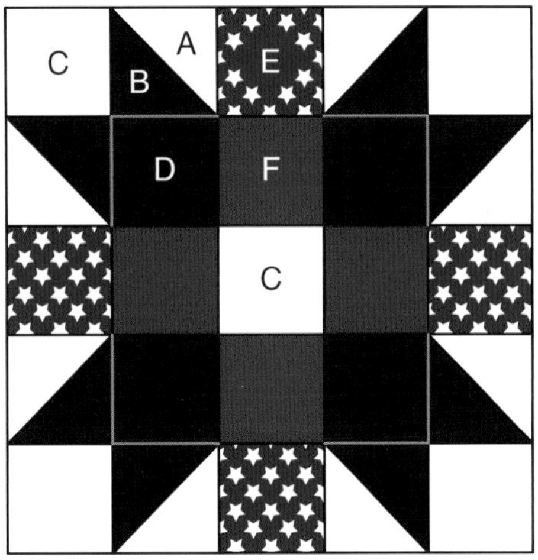

Large Star
10" x 10" Finished Block
Make 1

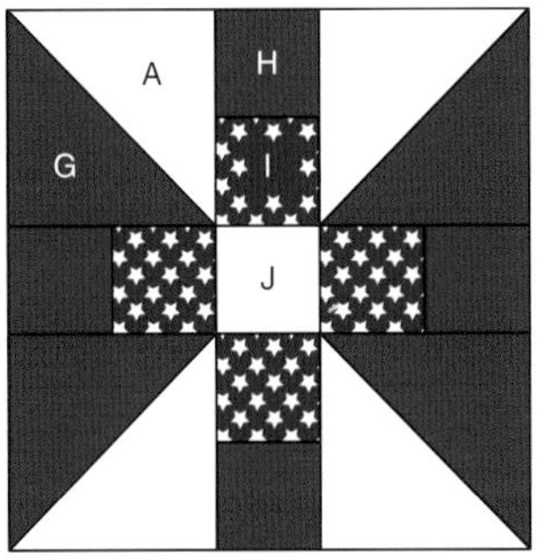

Propeller
5" x 5" Finished Block
Make 8

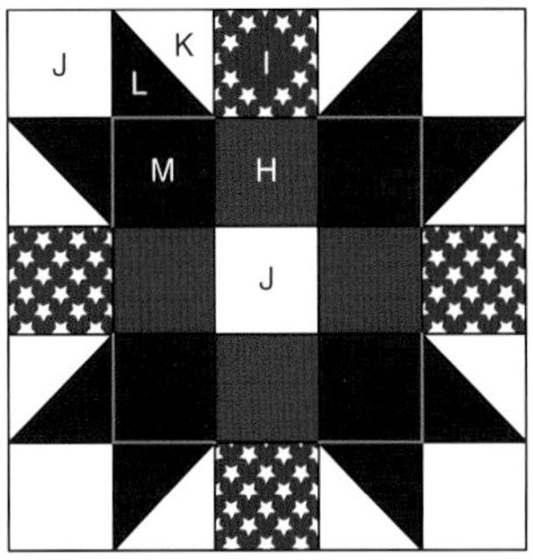

Small Star
5" x 5" Finished Block
Make 8

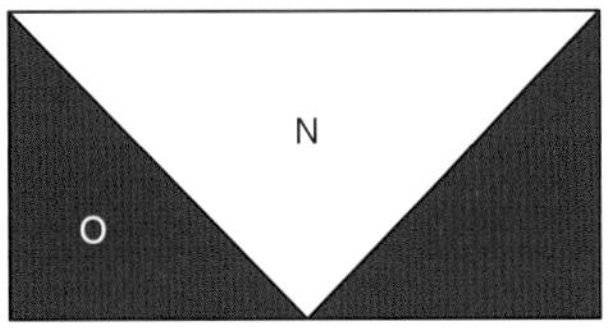

Flying Geese
2½" x 5" Finished Block
Make 20

Skill Level

Confident Beginner

Finished Sizes

Quilt Size: 35" x 35"
Block Sizes: 10" x 10", 5" x 5" and 2½" x 5"
Number of Blocks: 1, 16 and 20

Materials

- ⅝ yard white solid
- ⅓ yard navy solid
- ¼ yard star print
- ⅝ yard red solid
- ⅞ yard navy print
- 1¼ yards backing
- 40" x 40" batting
- Basic sewing tools and supplies

Project Notes

Read all instructions before beginning this project.

Stitch right sides together using a ¼" seam allowance unless otherwise specified.

Materials and cutting lists assume 40" of usable fabric width for yardage.

Arrows indicate directions to press seams.

WOF – width of fabric
HST – half-square triangle ⧅
QST – quarter-square triangle ⊠

Inspiration

"I love the bold contrast of this quilt. The stars stand out and are accentuated by the red zigzag pattern of the pieced border." —Joy Heimark

Cutting

From white solid cut:

- 5 (6¼") N squares
- 20 (3") A squares
- 5 (2½") C squares
- 32 (2") K squares
- 48 (1½") J squares

From navy solid cut:

- 4 (3") B squares
- 4 (2½") D squares
- 32 (2") L squares
- 32 (1½") M squares

From star print cut:

- 4 (2½") E squares
- 64 (1½") I squares

From red solid cut:

- 20 (3⅜") O squares
- 20 (3") G squares
- 4 (2½") F squares
- 64 (1½") H squares

From navy print cut:

- 5 (3" x WOF) strips, stitch short ends to short ends, then subcut into:
  2 (3" x 35½") S, 2 (3" x 30½") R, 2 (3" x 15½") Q and 2 (3" x 10½") P border strips
- 4 (2½" x WOF) binding strips

Completing the Blocks

1. Refer to Half-Square Triangles on page 16 and use four each of the A and B squares to make eight A-B units (Figure 1). Trim each unit to 2½" square, centering the diagonal seams.

A-B Unit
Make & trim 8

Figure 1

2. Using the A-B units and C, D, E and F squares as shown, arrange five rows of five squares/units each (Figure 2). Sew the rows and then sew the rows together to make a Large Star block.

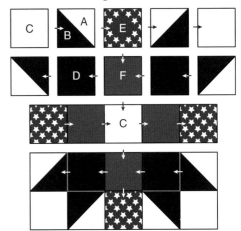

Make 1

Figure 2

3. Again referring to Half-Square Triangles, use 16 each of the A and G squares to make 32 A-G units (Figure 3). Trim each unit to 2½" square, centering seams.

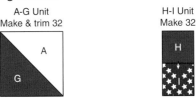

A-G Unit
Make & trim 32

Figure 3

H-I Unit
Make 32

Figure 4

4. Join an H and an I square to make an H-I unit (Figure 4). Make 32 H-I units.

5. Arrange four A-G units, four H-I units and a J square into three rows (Figure 5). Sew the rows and then sew the rows together to make a Propeller block. Make eight Propeller blocks.

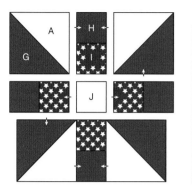

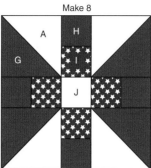

Make 8

Figure 5

6. Again referring to Half-Square Triangles, use the K and L squares to make 64 K-L units (Figure 6). Trim each unit to 1½" square, centering seams.

K-L Unit
Make & trim 64

Figure 6

7. Using the K-L units and H, I, J and M squares as shown, arrange five rows of five squares/units each (Figure 7). Sew the rows and then sew the rows together to make a Small Star block. Make eight Small Star blocks.

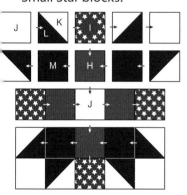

Make 8

Figure 7

8. Refer to Four-At-A-Time Flying Geese on page 16 and use the N and O squares to make 20 Flying Geese blocks (Figure 8).

Make 20

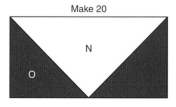

Figure 8

Completing the Quilt

1. Referring to the Assembly Diagram, sew the P strips to opposite sides of the Large Star block. Sew the Q strips to the top and bottom.

2. Watching orientation carefully, sew Propeller blocks to opposite sides of a Small Star block to make a side border. Make two. Sew to the sides of the quilt.

3. Watching orientation, join three Small Star blocks and two Propeller blocks, alternating, to make a top/bottom border. Make two. Sew to the top and bottom of the quilt.

4. Join five Flying Geese blocks to make a flying geese border. Make four. Sew two to the sides of the quilt. Add a G square to each end of each remaining flying geese border. Sew to the top and bottom of the quilt.

5. Sew the R and S border strips to the quilt top in alphabetical order.

6. Layer, baste, quilt as desired and bind referring to Quilting Basics. The red solid and navy print areas of the photographed quilt were quilted with a meander design. ●

American Pride
Assembly Diagram 35" x 35"

HALF-SQUARE TRIANGLES

Half-square triangles (HSTs) are a basic unit of quilting used in many blocks or on their own. This construction method will yield two HSTs.

1. Refer to the pattern for size to cut squares. The standard formula is to add ⅞" to the finished size of the square. Cut two squares from different colors this size. For example, for a 3" finished HST unit, cut 3⅞" squares.

2. Draw a diagonal line from corner to corner on the wrong side of the lightest color square. Layer the squares right sides together. Stitch ¼" on either side of the drawn line (Figure A).

Figure A

3. Cut the squares apart on the drawn line, leaving a ¼" seam allowance and making two HST units referring to Figure B.

Figure B

4. Open the HST units and press seam allowances toward the darker fabric making two HST units (Figure C). ●

Figure C

FOUR-AT-A-TIME FLYING GEESE

With this method, smaller squares are sewn onto opposite ends of a larger square. The unit is cut in half and additional small squares are sewn on the units. After sewing in place and cutting, the small squares are flipped open to create the flying geese unit.

The large square will be the center of the flying geese units, and the small squares will become the "wings." The bias edges aren't exposed until after sewing, so there is no concern about stretch and distortion (Photo A).

Photo A

Cutting
Refer to the pattern for the sizes to cut the rectangle and squares. Cut as directed in the pattern.

Determine the finished size of the flying geese unit you'd like to make and add 1¼" to the desired finished width of the flying geese unit, then cut one center square.

Add ⅞" to the height of the desired finished flying geese unit and cut four squares.

For example, to make four 2" x 4" finished flying geese units, cut one 5¼" square and four 2⅞" squares.

Assembly
1. Draw a diagonal line on the wrong side of each small square. Orienting the drawn lines as shown in photo, position two small squares on opposite corners of the large square. The small squares will overlap slightly in the middle. Stitch ¼" away from both sides of the marked line. Using a rotary cutter, cut on the marked line to create two units (Photo B).

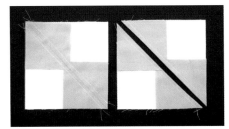

Photo B

2. Press seam allowances toward the small triangles.

3. Position the remaining squares on the units as shown and stitch ¼" away on each side of the marked line (Photo C).

Photo C

4. Cut on the marked line and press toward the triangles to create a total of four flying geese units (Photo D).

Photo D

5. If desired, trim dog-ears and square up the finished unit to the required unfinished size. ●

Fireworks & Stars

Stars and stripes are paired together to make this fun and patriotic wall hanging.

Designed & Quilted by Andy Knowlton of A Bright Corner

Skill Level
Confident Beginner

Finished Sizes
Wall Hanging Size: 34" x 34"
Block Size: 10" x 10"
Number of Blocks: 8

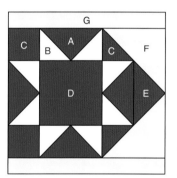

Block A
10" x 10" Finished Block
Make 4

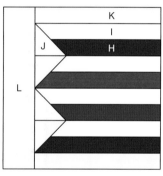

Block B
10" x 10" Finished Block
Make 4

Materials
- ⅝ yard medium blue print
- ¼ yard white print
- 4 (7" x 9") red scraps
- 4 (7" x 9") white scraps
- 1⅓ yard light blue print
- ⅜ yard dark blue print
- 1¼ yards backing
- 38" x 38" batting
- Basic sewing tools and supplies

Project Notes
Read all instructions before beginning this project.

Stitch right sides together using a ¼" seam allowance unless otherwise specified.

Materials and cutting lists assume 40" of usable fabric width.

Arrows indicate directions to press seams.

WOF – width of fabric
HST – half-square triangle ◻
QST – quarter-square triangle ⊠

Cutting

From medium blue print cut:
- 4 (4½") D squares
- 4 (2½" x 8½") E rectangles
- 16 (2½" x 4½") A rectangles
- 16 (2½") C squares

From white print cut:
- 32 (2½") B squares

From red scraps cut:
- 16 (1½" x 8½") H rectangles

From white scraps cut:
- 16 (1½" x 8½") I rectangles

From light blue print cut:
- 1 (10½") M square
- 8 (4½") F squares
- 16 (2½") J squares
- 4 (2½" x 10½") L rectangles
- 2 (2" x 30½") N border strips
- 2 (2" x 34½") O border strips
- 8 (1½" x 10½") G rectangles
- 8 (1½" x 8½") K rectangles

From dark blue print cut:
- 4 (2½" x WOF) binding strips

Inspiration

"One of our favorite summertime events is to go to our local community parade and fireworks show in early June. It's a great way to kick off the summer and it has become one our family traditions!" —Andy Knowlton

Completing the Blocks

1. Refer to Sew & Flip Flying Geese and use A rectangles and B squares to make 16 A-B units (Figure 1).

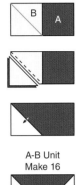

A-B Unit
Make 16

Figure 1

2. Lay out four A-B units, four C squares and one D square into three rows and sew together. Join rows together to make star unit (Figure 2). Make four.

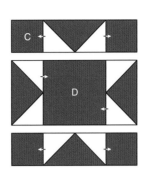

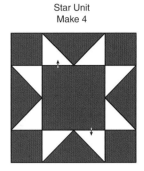

Star Unit
Make 4

Figure 2

SEW & FLIP FLYING GEESE

With this method, squares are sewn onto opposite ends of a rectangle. The rectangle will be the center of the flying geese unit and the squares will become the "wings." After sewing in place, the squares are trimmed and flipped open to create the unit. The bias edges aren't exposed until after sewing so there is no concern about stretch and distortion.

Cutting

Refer to the pattern for the sizes to cut the rectangle and squares. Cut as directed in the pattern.

Determine the finished size of the flying geese unit you'd like to make and add ½" to the desired finished height and width of the flying geese unit, then cut a rectangle that size.

Cut two squares the same size as the height of the cut rectangle.

For example, to make one 2" x 4" finished flying geese unit, cut a 2½" x 4½" rectangle and two 2½" squares (Photo A).

Photo A

Assembly

1. Draw a diagonal line from corner to corner on the wrong side of each small square.

Place a square, right sides together, on one end of the rectangle. Sew just outside the drawn line (Photo B).

Photo B

2. Using a rotary cutter, trim ¼" away from sewn line.

Open and press to reveal the corner triangle or wing (Photo C).

Photo C

3. Place the second square, right sides together, on the opposite end of the rectangle. This square will slightly overlap the previous piece.

Sew just outside the drawn line and trim ¼" away from sewn line as before.

Open and press to complete the flying geese unit (Photo D).

Photo D

4. If desired, square up the finished unit to the required unfinished size. ●

3. Sew an E rectangle to the right edge of a star unit (Figure 3). Make four.

Make 4

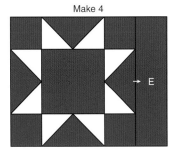

Figure 3

4. Refer again to Sew & Flip Corners and sew two F squares to the right edge of a star unit (Figure 4). Make four.

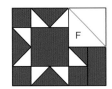

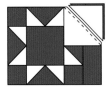

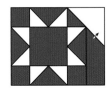

Make 4

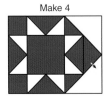

Figure 4

5. Sew a G rectangle to the top and bottom of a star unit to complete one Block A (Figure 5). Make four.

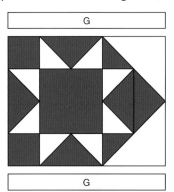

Block A
Make 4

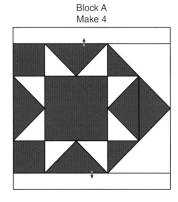

Figure 5

6. Sew one H rectangle and one I rectangle together along the long edge to make a strip pair (Figure 6). Make 16.

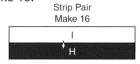

Strip Pair
Make 16

Figure 6

7. Refer again to Sew & Flip Corners to add J squares to the left edges of each strip pair. Note that the white rectangle is on the top, and pay attention to the orientation of the corner triangles (Figure 7).

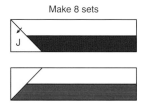

Make 8 sets

Figure 7

8. Sew four strip pairs together to make a strip unit (Figure 8). Make four.

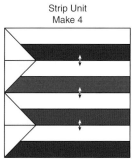

Strip Unit
Make 4

Figure 8

9. Sew one K rectangle to the top and bottom of a strip unit and one L rectangle to the left edge to complete one Block B (Figure 9). Make four.

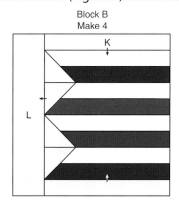

Block B
Make 4

Figure 9

Completing the Wall Hanging

1. Referring to the Assembly Diagram, lay out the A and B blocks and M square into three rows of three blocks each, rotating blocks as shown. Sew the blocks together in rows; join the rows to complete the wall hanging center.

2. Sew the N and O border strips to the wall hanging top in alphabetical order.

3. Layer, baste, quilt as desired and bind referring to Quilting Basics. The photographed wall hanging was quilted with an allover orange peel design. ●

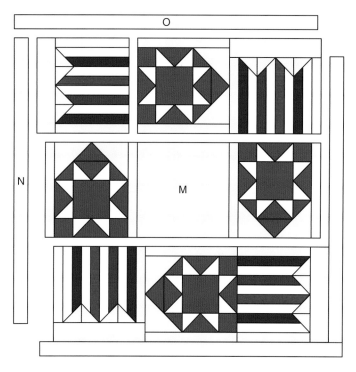

Fireworks Stars
Assembly Diagram 34" x 34"

Blooming Pumpkins

The combination of the pumpkins and blossoming flowers in this wall hanging creates a captivating autumnal display that would add warmth and vibrancy to any room.

Design by Roni Hickey
Quilted by Bobbi Clark of Valley Fabric Shop

Skill Level
Confident Beginner

Finished Sizes
Wall Hanging Size: 22" x 46"
Block Size: 10" x 10"
Number of Blocks: 3

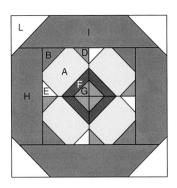

Dark Pumpkin
10" x 10" Finished Block
Make 2

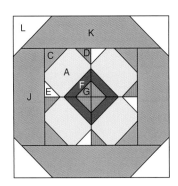

Light Pumpkin
10" x 10" Finished Block
Make 1

Materials
- ⅝ yard cream tone on tone
- ⅓ yard gold print
- ⅛ yard gold solid
- ⅛ yard green print
- ⅛ yard medium brown plaid
- ⅓ yard dark orange print
- ¼ yard orange print
- ⅝ yard dark brown print
- ½ yard floral print
- 1⅜ yards backing
- 26" x 50" batting
- Template material
- ¼ yard 17"-wide lightweight paper-backed fusible web
- Thread
- Basic sewing tools and supplies

Project Notes
Read all instructions before beginning this project.

Stitch right sides together using a ¼" seam allowance unless otherwise specified.

Materials and cutting lists assume 40" of usable fabric width for yardage.

Arrows indicate directions to press seams.

Appliqué patterns are reversed for fusible appliqué.

WOF – width of fabric
HST – half-square triangle ◻
QST – quarter-square triangle ⊠

Inspiration

"I was inspired to design this wall hanging by the beauty of nature during the autumn season. The vibrant colors of the changing leaves and the abundance of pumpkins and flowers served as a visual inspiration. I wanted to capture that essence in a cozy and decorative piece that would bring warmth and a touch of nature into any home." —Roni Hickey

Cutting

From cream tone on tone cut:
- 12 (3") L squares
- 2 (2½" x 38½") N rectangles
- 4 (2½" x 10½") M rectangles
- 12 (1½") E squares

From gold print cut:
- 12 (3½") A squares

From gold solid cut:
- 12 (1½") G squares

From green print cut:
- 12 (1½") D squares

From medium brown plaid cut:
- 12 (2¼") F squares

From dark orange print cut:
- 4 (2½" x 10½") I rectangles
- 4 (2½" x 6½") H rectangles
- 8 (2") B squares

From orange print cut:
- 2 (2½" x 10½") K rectangles
- 2 (2½" x 6½") J rectangles
- 4 (2") C squares

From dark brown print cut:
- 2 (1½" x 38½") O strips
- 2 (1½" x 14½") P strips
- 4 (2½" x WOF) binding strips

From floral print cut:
- 4 (3½" x WOF) strips, stitch short ends to short ends, then subcut into:
    2 (3½" x 40½") Q strips and
    2 (3½"x 22½") R strips

Completing the Blocks

A-D-E Unit
Make 12

1. Refer to Sew & Flip Corners on page 8 and sew D squares to the upper right corners and E squares to the lower left corners of the A squares to make 12 A-D-E units (Figure 1).

Figure 1

2. In the same manner, sew F squares to the lower right corners of the A-D-E units (Figure 2a). Repeat to sew G squares to the F squares (Figure 2b).

a. Make 12   b. Make 12

Figure 2

3. In the same manner, sew a B square to the upper left corner of eight step 2 units to make dark units (Figure 3a). Repeat using C squares to make four light units (Figure 3b).

Dark Unit
a. Make 8

Light Unit
b. Make 4

Figure 3

4. Arrange and sew together groups of four dark units as shown to make two dark flower units (Figure 4a). Repeat with light units to make one light flower unit (Figure 4b).

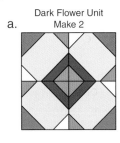

Dark Flower Unit
a. Make 2

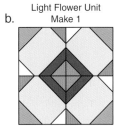

Light Flower Unit
b. Make 1

Figure 4

5. Sew H rectangles to opposite sides of the dark flower units; sew I rectangles to the top and bottom (Figure 5a). Repeat with light flower unit, J rectangles and K rectangles (Figure 5b).

a.

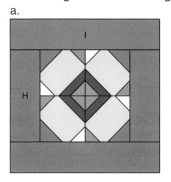

b.

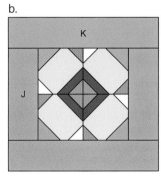

Figure 5

6. Refer to Sew & Flip Corners and the Dark and Light Pumpkin block diagrams and sew L squares to the corners of the step 5 units to make two Dark Pumpkin blocks and one Light Pumpkin block.

Completing the Wall Hanging

1. Refer to the Assembly Diagram and sew together the blocks and M strips alternately in a vertical row; sew the N strips to opposite long sides of the wall hanging center.

2. Sew the borders to the wall hanging center in alphabetical order to complete the wall hanging top.

3. Layer, baste, quilt wall hanging as desired and bind referring to Quilting Basics. The photographed wall hanging was stitched in the ditch and straight line echo quilted.

4. Prepare templates for the stem, large leaf and small leaf using the patterns provided. Refer to Raw-Edge Fusible Appliqué on page 26 and prepare the appliqué shapes as follows:
• Green print – 3 large leaves, 3 small leaves
• Dark brown print – 3 stems

5. Refer to the photo and place one of each large leaf, small leaf and stem on each pumpkin. When satisfied, fuse in place referring to manufacturer's instructions. Straight-stitch along edge of stem and add veins to leaves using matching threads to complete the wall hanging. ●

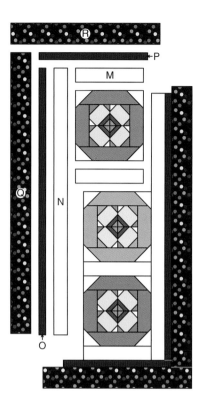

Blooming Pumpkins
Assembly Diagram 22" x 46"

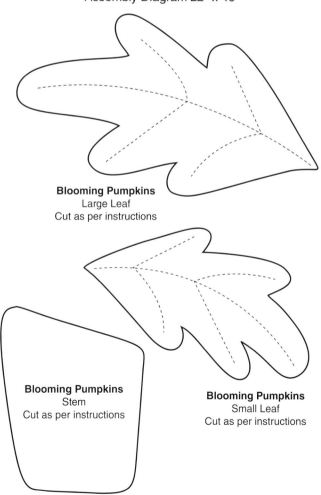

Blooming Pumpkins
Large Leaf
Cut as per instructions

Blooming Pumpkins
Stem
Cut as per instructions

Blooming Pumpkins
Small Leaf
Cut as per instructions

RAW-EDGE FUSIBLE APPLIQUÉ

One of the easiest ways to appliqué is the raw-edge fusible-web method. Individual pieces of paper-backed fusible web are fused to the wrong side of specified fabrics, cut out and then fused together in a motif or individually to a foundation fabric, where they are machine-stitched in place.

Choosing Appliqué Fabrics

Depending on the appliqué, you may want to consider using batiks. Batik is a much tighter weave and, because of the manufacturing process, does not fray. If you are thinking about using regular quilting cottons, be sure to stitch your raw-edge appliqués with blanket/buttonhole stitches instead of a straight stitch.

Cutting Appliqué Pieces

1. Fusible appliqué shapes should be reversed for this technique.

2. Trace the appliqué shapes onto the paper side of paper-backed fusible web. Leave at least ¼" between shapes. Cut out shapes leaving a margin around traced lines. **Note:** *If doing several identical appliqués, trace reversed shapes onto template material to make reusable templates for tracing shapes onto the fusible web.*

3. Follow manufacturer's instructions and fuse shapes to wrong side of fabric as indicated on pattern for color and number to cut.

4. Cut out appliqué shapes on traced lines. Remove paper backing from shapes.

5. Again following fusible web manufacturer's instructions, arrange and fuse pieces to quilt referring to quilt pattern. Or fuse together shapes on top of an appliqué ironing mat to make an appliqué motif that can then be fused to the quilt.

Stitching Appliqué Edges

Machine-stitch appliqué edges to secure the appliqués in place and help finish the raw edges with matching or invisible thread (Photo A). **Note:** *To show stitching, all samples have been stitched with contrasting thread.*

Photo A — Straight stitch

Invisible thread can be used to stitch appliqués down when using the blanket or straight stitches. Do not use it for the satin stitch. Definitely practice with invisible thread before using it on your quilt; it can sometimes be difficult to work with.

A short, narrow buttonhole or blanket stitch is most commonly used (Photo B). Your machine manual may also refer to this as an appliqué stitch. Be sure to stitch next to the appliqué edge with the stitch catching the appliqué.

Photo B — Buttonhole or blanket stitch

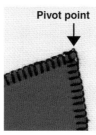
Photo C — Pivot point

Practice turning inside and outside corners on scrap fabric before stitching appliqué pieces. Learn how your machine stitches so that you can make the pivot points smooth (Photo C).

1. To stitch outer corners, stitch to the edge of the corner and stop with needle in the fabric at the corner point. Pivot to the next side of the corner and continue to sew (Photo D). You will get a box on an outside corner.

Photo D

2. To stitch inner corners, pivot at the inner point with needle in fabric (Photo E). You will see a Y shape in the corner.

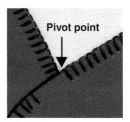
Photo E — Pivot point

3. You can also use a machine straight stitch. Turn corners in the same manner, stitching to the corners and pivoting with needle in down position (Photos F and G).

Photo F   **Photo G**

General Appliqué Tips

1. Use a light- to medium-weight stabilizer behind an appliqué to keep the fabric from puckering during machine stitching (Photo H).

Photo H

2. To reduce the stiffness of a finished appliqué, cut out the center of the fusible web shape, leaving ¼"–½" inside the pattern line. This gives a border of adhesive to fuse to the background and leaves the center soft and easy to quilt.

3. If an appliqué fabric is so light colored or thin that the background fabric shows through, fuse a lightweight interfacing to the wrong side of the fabric. You can also fuse a piece of the appliqué fabric to a matching piece, wrong sides together, and then apply the fusible web with a drawn pattern to one side. ●

Sasha Mae

Kittens hiding among granny squares create a cozy autumn throw.

Designed & Quilted by Jill Metzger

Skill Level
Confident Beginner

Finished Sizes
Quilt Size: 45" x 58"
Block Size: 11" x 11"
Number of Blocks: 12

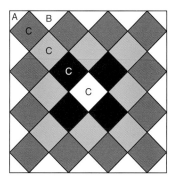

Big Granny Block
11" x 11" Finished Block
Make 6

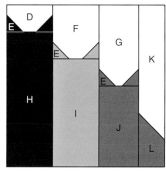

Three Kittens
11" x 11" Finished Block
Make 6

Materials
- 1¾ yards white solid
- 6 fat quarters black print
- 6 fat quarters yellow print
- 6 fat quarters orange print
- ⅝ yard orange print for border
- ⅝ yard black print for binding
- 3 yards backing
- 53" x 66" batting
- Basic sewing tools and supplies

Project Notes
Read all instructions before beginning this project.

Stitch right sides together using a ¼" seam allowance unless otherwise specified.

Materials and cutting lists assume 40" of usable fabric width for yardage and 20" for fat quarters.

Arrows indicate directions to press seams.

WOF – width of fabric
HST – half-square triangle ◹
QST – quarter-square triangle ⊠

Cutting

From white solid cut:
- 18 (4") B squares, then cut twice diagonally ⊠
- 2 (3½" x WOF) strips, subcut into:
    6 (3½" x 6½") G rectangles
    6 (3½" x 4½") F rectangles
- 11 (2½" x WOF) strips, subcut into:
    32 (2½" x 11½") M rectangles
    6 (2½" x 10⅞") K rectangles
    6 (2½" x 3½") D rectangles
    6 (2½") C squares
- 12 (2¼") A squares, then cut once diagonally ◹

From each black print fat quarter cut:
- 1 (3½" x 9½") H rectangle
- 8 (2½") C squares
- 2 (1⅞") E squares

From each yellow print fat quarter cut:
- 1 (3½" x 7½") I rectangle
- 8 (2½") C squares
- 2 (1⅞") E squares

From each orange print fat quarter cut:
- 1 (3½" x 5½") J rectangle
- 1 (2½" x 3⅞") L rectangle
- 12 (2½") C squares
- 2 (1⅞") E squares

From orange print cut:
- 6 (2½" x WOF) strips, stitch short ends to short ends, then subcut into:
    2 (2½" x 41½") N and 2 (2½" x 58½") O border strips

Completing the Blocks

1. Using white A and B triangles and one set each of black print, yellow print and orange print C squares, sew into rows as shown. Join rows together to make one Big Granny Block (Figure 1). Make six.

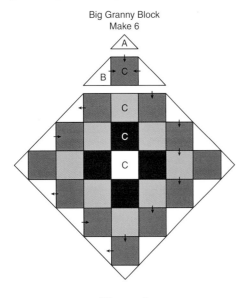

Big Granny Block
Make 6

Figure 1

2. Refer to Sew & Flip Corners on page 8 and use a white D rectangle and two matching black E squares to make one black kitten ear unit (Figure 2). Make six.

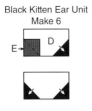

Black Kitten Ear Unit
Make 6

Figure 2

3. In the same manner, use a white F rectangle and two matching yellow E squares to make one yellow kitten ear unit (Figure 3). Make six.

Yellow Kitten Ear Unit
Make 6

Figure 3

4. In the same manner, use a white G rectangle and two matching orange E squares to make one orange kitten ear unit (Figure 4). Make six.

Orange Kitten Ear Unit
Make 6

Figure 4

5. Referring again to Sew & Flip corners, join a white K and an orange L rectangle at a right angle as shown to make an orange kitten body unit (Figure 5). Make six.

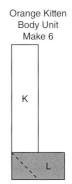

Orange Kitten
Body Unit
Make 6

Figure 5

6. Sew black kitten ear units to matching black H rectangles to complete six black kitten units. Repeat to make six yellow kitten units with I rectangles and six orange kitten units with J rectangles (Figure 6).

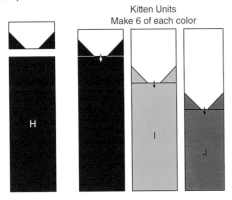

Kitten Units
Make 6 of each color

Figure 6

7. Referring to Figure 7, join three kitten units and one matching orange kitten body unit together as shown to make one Three Kittens block. Make six.

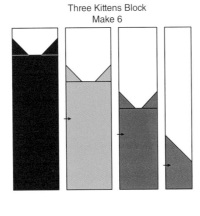

Three Kittens Block
Make 6

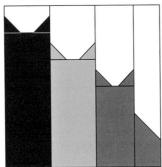

Figure 7

Completing the Quilt

1. Referring to the Assembly Diagram, lay out four black C squares and three white M rectangles. Sew to make one sashing row. Make five. ***Note:*** *You will have leftover black C squares.*

2. Lay out blocks, white M rectangles and sashing rows in nine rows, noting the placement of the blocks. Sew together. Join the rows to complete the quilt center. Press.

3. Sew the N and O border strips to the quilt top in alphabetical order.

4. Layer, baste, quilt as desired and bind referring to Quilting Basics. The photographed quilt was hand-quilted with an outline stitch and black embroidery floss. ●

Sasha Mae
Assembly Diagram 45" x 48"

Pumpkin Boo!

Feature cats and pumpkins for fun Halloween decor.

Designed & Quilted by Wendy Sheppard

Skill Level
Confident Beginner

Finished Sizes
Pillow Size: 22" x 14"
Block Size: 6" x 12"
Number of Blocks: 3

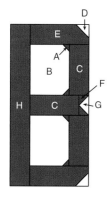

B
6" x 12" Finished Block
Make 1

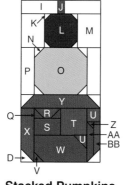

Stacked Pumpkins
6" x 12" Finished Block
Make 2

Materials

- ⅛ yard brown leaf print*
- ¾ yard white print*
- ⅛ yard brown dot*
- 1 (4") square orange print #1*
- ⅜ yard orange print #2*
- ⅛ yard orange print #3*
- 1 (4") square orange print #4*
- 1 (5") square orange print #5*
- ⅛ yard orange print #6*
- 16" x 24" muslin
- 16" x 24" batting*
- 22" x 14" pillow form
- Thread*
- Basic sewing tools and supplies

*Fabrics from the Awesome Autumn collection by Sandy Gervais and the Bee Cross Stitch collection by Lori Holt for Riley Blake Designs; Tuscan silk batting from Hobbs Bonded Fibers; 50 wt. Mako thread from Aurifil used to make sample. EQ8 was used to design this pillow.

Project Notes

Read all instructions before beginning this project.

Stitch right sides together using a ¼" seam allowance unless otherwise specified.

Materials and cutting lists assume 40" of usable fabric width for yardage.

Arrows indicate directions to press seams.

WOF – width of fabric
HST – half-square triangle ◺
QST – quarter-square triangle ⊠

Cutting

From brown leaf print cut:

- 1 (2" x 12½") H rectangle
- 2 (2" x 5") E rectangles
- 3 (2" x 4¼") C rectangles
- 2 (1¼") F squares
- 4 (1") A squares

From white print cut:

- 2 (14½") EE squares
- 2 (3½" x 4¼") B rectangles
- 4 (2¼" x 3") M rectangles
- 2 (1½" x 22½") DD rectangles
- 4 (1½" x 12½") CC rectangles
- 4 (1½" x 4") P rectangles
- 4 (1½" x 3¼") I rectangles
- 10 (1½") D squares
- 1 (1¼" x 2") G rectangle
- 8 (1¼") N squares
- 8 (1") K squares

From brown dot cut:

- 2 (2½" x 4½") W rectangles
- 2 (1¾" x 2½") S rectangles
- 4 (1¼") Q squares
- 2 (1" x 3½") AA rectangles
- 2 (1" x 1½") J rectangles

From each of orange prints #1 and #4 cut:

- 1 (3") L square

From orange print #2 cut:

- 3 (2½" x WOF) binding strips
- 1 (4" x 4½") O rectangle

From each of orange prints #3 and #6 cut:

- 1 (2½") T square
- 1 (1½" x 6½") Y rectangle
- 1 (1½" x 4½") X rectangle
- 2 (1½") U squares
- 1 (1¼" x 2½") R rectangle
- 1 (1¼") V square
- 1 (1" x 3½") BB rectangle
- 1 (1") Z square

From orange print #5 cut:

- 1 (4" x 4½") O rectangle

Completing the B Block

1. Refer to Sew & Flip Corners on page 8 and add two A squares to a B rectangle (Figure 1a). Sew to a C rectangle to make an A-B-C unit (Figure 1b). Make two.

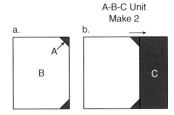

A-B-C Unit
Make 2

Figure 1

2. Use the sew and flip technique to add a D square to an E rectangle (Figure 2). Make two D-E units, one of each orientation.

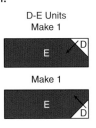

D-E Units
Make 1

Make 1

Figure 2

3. Use the sew and flip technique to add two F squares to a G rectangle (Figure 3a). Sew to a C rectangle to make an F-G-C unit (Figure 3b).

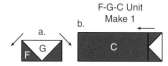

F-G-C Unit
Make 1

Figure 3

4. Join the D-E units, A-B-C units, and F-G-C unit (Figure 4). Sew an H rectangle to the left side to complete the B block.

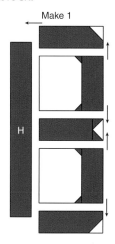

Make 1

Figure 4

Completing the Stacked Pumpkins Blocks

1. Sew I rectangles to opposite sides of a J rectangle to make a stem unit (Figure 5). Make two.

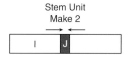

Stem Unit
Make 2

Figure 5

2. Use the sew and flip technique to add four K squares to an L square (Figure 6a). Sew M rectangles to opposite sides to complete a top pumpkin (Figure 6b). Make two.

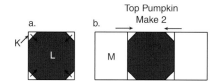

Top Pumpkin
Make 2

Figure 6

3. Use the sew and flip technique to add four N squares to an O rectangle (Figure 7a). Sew P rectangles to opposite sides to complete a middle pumpkin (Figure 7b). Make two.

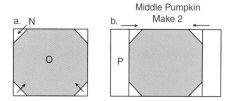

Middle Pumpkin
Make 2

Figure 7

Note: *For steps 4–7, use matching orange #3 or orange #6 pieces.*

4. Use the sew and flip technique to add two Q squares to an R rectangle (Figure 8a). Sew an S rectangle to the bottom and a T square to the right side to complete the cat head unit (Figure 8b).

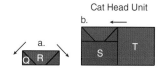

Cat Head Unit

Figure 8

5. Use the sew and flip technique to add a U square and a V square to a W rectangle to make the cat body unit (Figure 9).

Cat Body Unit

Figure 9

6. In the same way, add D squares to an X rectangle (Figure 10) and a Y rectangle (Figure 11).

Figure 10

Figure 11

7. Use the sew and flip technique to add a Z square to an AA rectangle (Figure 12a). Sew a BB rectangle to the right side (Figure 12b). Use the sew and flip technique to add a D square to the unit (Figure 12c). Sew a U square to the top to complete the tail unit (Figure 12d).

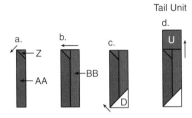

Figure 12

8. Join the cat head unit to the cat body unit (Figure 13). Sew the tail unit to the right side. Sew the Figure 10 unit to the left and the Figure 11 unit to the top to complete a bottom pumpkin.

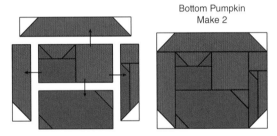

Bottom Pumpkin
Make 2

Figure 13

9. Repeat steps 4–8 to make a second bottom pumpkin.

10. Join a stem unit, top pumpkin, middle pumpkin, and bottom pumpkin to complete a Stacked Pumpkins block (Figure 14). Make two.

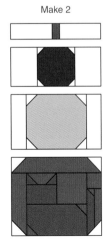

Make 2

Figure 14

Completing the Pillow

1. Referring to the Assembly Diagram, sew four CC rectangles and the blocks together, alternating. Sew the DD rectangles to the top and bottom to complete the pillow top.

2. Layer the pillow top with the batting and muslin rectangles, baste and quilt, referring to Quilting Basics. The photographed pillow top was quilted with a swirl design. Trim to 22½" x 14½".

3. Fold under ¼" on an edge of an EE square, followed by another fold of about 1". Sew the fold in place. Repeat for the other EE square.

4. Layer the pillow top, right side down, and the hemmed EE squares, right sides up with hemmed edges in the middle and outer raw edges aligned with the pillow top. Pin together and then sew around the pillow top. Bind the edges, referring to Quilting Basics. Insert the pillow form. ●

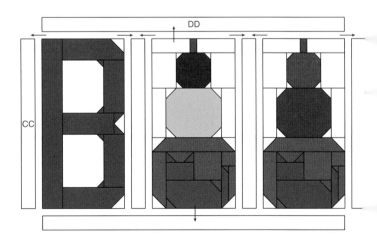

Pumpkin Boo!
Assembly Diagram 22" x 14"

Tree Farm

Quick-to-complete tree blocks make a fun small throw.

Design by Wendy Sheppard
Quilted by Darlene Szabo of Sew Graceful Quilting

Skill Level
Confident Beginner

Finished Sizes
Quilt Size: 44" x 55"
Block Size: 8" x 9"
Number of Blocks: 23

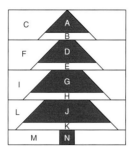

Tree
8" x 9" Finished Block
Make 23

Materials
- 1 fat quarter each 5 assorted red prints*
- 1 fat eighth each 4 assorted green prints*
- 3 yards ivory solid*
- ½ yard light green print*
- 3⅛ yards backing
- 52" x 63" batting*
- Basic sewing tools and supplies
- Thread*

Fabrics from the A Christmas Carol collection by 3 Sisters for Moda Fabrics; Tuscany silk batting from Hobbs Bonded Fibers; 50 wt. Mako thread from Aurifil used to make sample. EQ8 was used to design this quilt.

Project Notes
Read all instructions before beginning this project.

Stitch right sides together using a ¼" seam allowance unless otherwise specified.

Materials and cutting lists assume 41" of usable fabric width for yardage and 20" for fat quarters and fat eighths.

Arrows indicate directions to press seams.

WOF – width of fabric
HST – half-square triangle ▢
QST – quarter-square triangle ⊠

Cutting

From each red print fat quarter cut:
- 3 (2" x 7½") J rectangles
- 3 (2" x 6½") G rectangles
- 3 (2" x 5½") D rectangles
- 3 (2" x 4½") A rectangles
- 3 (1½") N squares

From each green print fat eighth cut:
- 2 (2" x 7½") J rectangles
- 2 (2" x 6½") G rectangles
- 2 (2" x 5½") D rectangles
- 2 (2" x 4½") A rectangles
- 2 (1½") N squares

From ivory solid cut:
- 4 (4½" x 9½") O rectangles
- 46 (2½" x 4½") C rectangles
- 46 (2½" x 4") F rectangles
- 46 (2½" x 3½") I rectangles
- 46 (2½" x 3") L rectangles
- 4 (2" x 40½") P strips
- 46 (1½" x 4") M rectangles
- 23 (1" x 7½") K rectangles
- 23 (1" x 6½") H rectangles
- 23 (1" x 5½") E rectangles
- 23 (1" x 4½") B rectangles
- 5 (2½" x WOF) strips, stitch short ends to short ends, then subcut into:
   2 (2½" x 51½") Q and 2 (2½" x 44½") R border strips

From light green print cut:
- 6 (2½" x WOF) binding strips

Completing the Blocks

1. Select a matching set of one each of the A, D, G and J rectangles plus a matching N square for the first block. Sew a B rectangle to the A rectangle to make an A-B unit (Figure 1a).

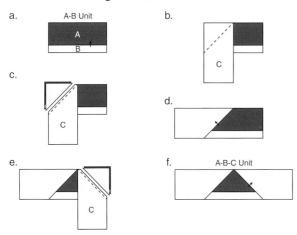

Figure 1

2. Draw a diagonal line on the wrong side of a C rectangle, watching orientation (Figure 1b). Place the marked rectangle on the A-B unit, right sides together. Sew on the marked line.

3. Trim ¼" away from the sewn line (Figure 1c). Press (Figure 1d).

4. Repeat the mark, sew, trim and press process to add a second C rectangle to the opposite end of the A-B unit. This completes an A-B-C unit (Figures 1e and 1f).

5. In the same way, make a D-E unit and add two F rectangles to complete a D-E-F unit (Figure 2).

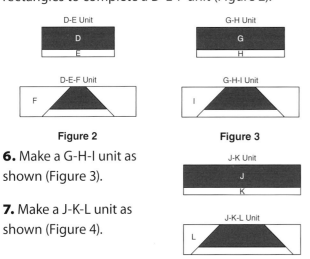

Figure 2

6. Make a G-H-I unit as shown (Figure 3).

7. Make a J-K-L unit as shown (Figure 4).

Figure 3

Figure 4

8. Sew M rectangles to opposite sides of the N square to make the trunk unit (Figure 5).

Trunk Unit

Figure 5

9. Join the matching A-B-C, D-E-F, G-H-I and J-K-L units (Figure 6). Add the trunk unit to complete a Tree block. Repeat steps 1–9 to make 15 red print blocks and eight green print blocks total.

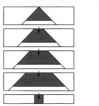
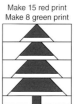

Make 15 red print
Make 8 green print

Figure 6

Completing the Quilt

1. Referring to the Assembly Diagram, lay out the red print blocks in three rows of five blocks each. Lay out the green print blocks in two rows of four blocks each. Add O rectangles to the ends of the green print block rows.

2. Sew the block rows. Join the rows and the four P strips, alternating, to complete the quilt center. Press.

3. Sew the Q and R border strips to the quilt top in alphabetical order.

4. Layer, baste, quilt as desired and bind referring to Quilting Basics. The photographed quilt was quilted with an edge-to-edge swirl design. ●

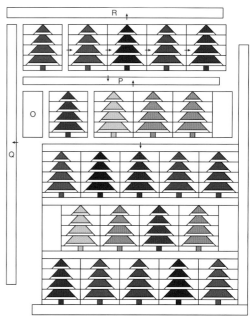

Tree Farm
Assembly Diagram 44" x 55"

Jolly Holiday

Add these festive St. Nicks to your holiday wall or table.

Designed & Quilted by Cathey Laird

Skill Level

Intermediate

Finished Sizes

Quilt Size: 45" x 45"
Block Size: 9" x 9"
Number of Blocks: 9

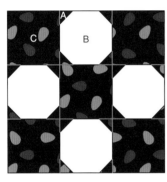

Pompoms
9" x 9" Finished Block
Make 1

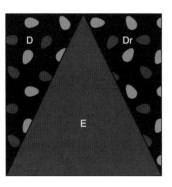

Hat
9" x 9" Finished Block
Make 4

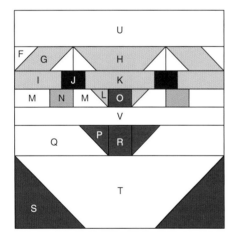

Face
9" x 9" Finished Block
Make 4

Materials

- 1½ yards black print*
- ½ yard white tone-on-tone*
- ½ yard red dot*
- ¼ yard beige tone-on-tone*
- 5" square black tone-on-tone*
- 5" square pink print*
- ⅛ yard red tone-on-tone*
- ½ yard red and white print*
- 3 yards backing
- 50" x 50" batting*
- Basic sewing tools and supplies
- Thread*

*Fabrics from the Jolly Holiday collection by Patrick Lose for Northcott; Warm & Natural cotton batting from The Warm Company; 50 wt. Mako thread from Aurifil used to make sample. EQ8 was used to design this quilt.

Project Notes

Read all instructions before beginning this project.

Stitch right sides together using a ¼" seam allowance unless otherwise specified.

Materials and cutting lists assume 40" of usable fabric width for yardage.

Arrows indicate directions to press seams.

WOF – width of fabric
HST – half-square triangle ◻
QST – quarter-square triangle ⊠

Cutting

From black print cut:

- 2 (10") X squares
- 8 (9½") Z squares
- 4 each D and D reversed (Dr) triangles
- 5 (3½") C squares
- 16 (1¼") A squares
- 5 (2½" x WOF) binding strips

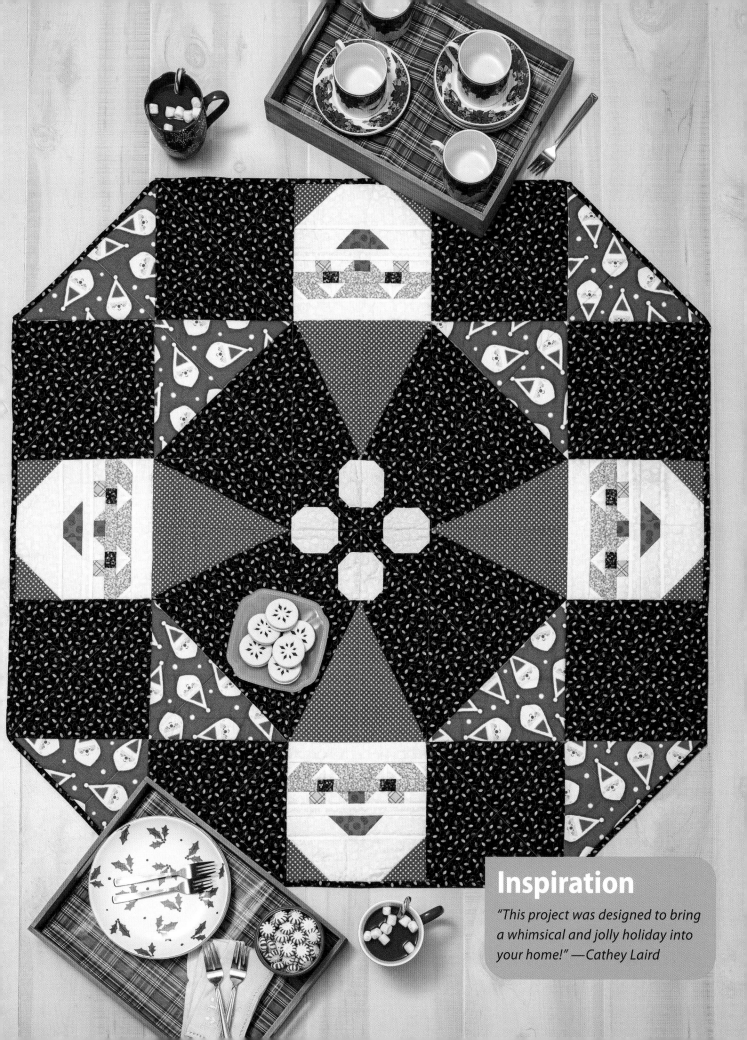

From white tone-on-tone cut:

- 4 (3½" x 9½") T rectangles
- 4 (3½") B squares
- 4 (2" x 9½") U rectangles
- 8 (1¾" x 4½") Q rectangles
- 24 (1½") F squares
- 4 (1¼" x 9½") V rectangles
- 16 (1¼" x 2") M rectangles

From red dot cut:

- 4 E triangles
- 8 (3½") S squares

From beige tone-on-tone cut:

- 4 (1½" x 4½") H rectangles
- 8 (1½" x 3") G rectangles
- 4 (1¼" x 3½") K rectangles
- 8 (1¼" x 2½") I rectangles
- 8 (1¼") L squares

From black tone-on-tone cut:

- 8 (1¼" x 1½") J rectangles

From pink print cut:

- 8 (1¼" x 1½") N rectangles

From red tone-on-tone cut:

- 8 (1¾") P squares
- 4 (1½" x 1¾") R rectangles
- 4 (1¼" x 1½") O rectangles

From red and white print cut:

- 1 (14") Y square, then cut twice diagonally ⊠
- 2 (10") W squares

Completing the Blocks & Units

1. Refer to Sew & Flip Corners on page 8 and use the A and B squares to make four A-B units (Figure 1).

A-B Unit
Make 4

Figure 1

2. Arrange and sew three rows using five C squares and the A-B units (Figure 2). Join the rows to complete the Pompoms block.

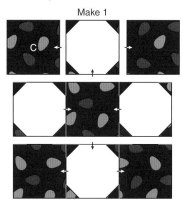

Make 1

Figure 2

3. Sew D and D reversed (Dr) triangles to an E triangle to make a Hat block (Figure 3). Make four Hat blocks.

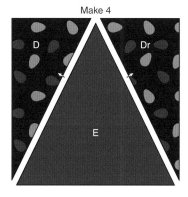

Make 4

Figure 3

4. Again using the sew-and-flip technique, make four each of the F-G, F-G reversed and F-H units (Figure 4).

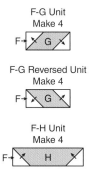

F-G Unit
Make 4

F-G Reversed Unit
Make 4

F-H Unit
Make 4

Figure 4

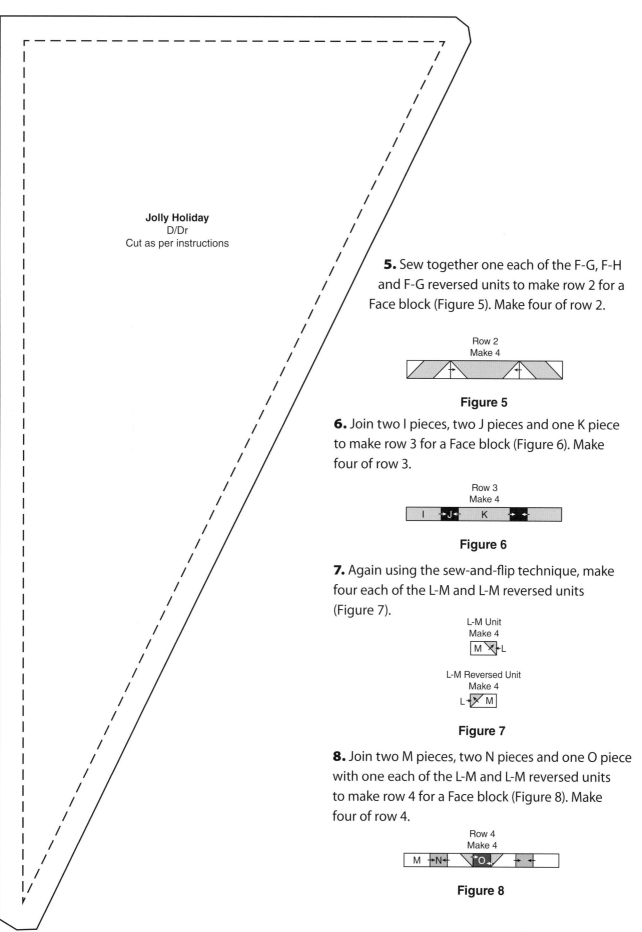

Jolly Holiday
D/Dr
Cut as per instructions

5. Sew together one each of the F-G, F-H and F-G reversed units to make row 2 for a Face block (Figure 5). Make four of row 2.

Row 2
Make 4

Figure 5

6. Join two I pieces, two J pieces and one K piece to make row 3 for a Face block (Figure 6). Make four of row 3.

Row 3
Make 4

I   J   K

Figure 6

7. Again using the sew-and-flip technique, make four each of the L-M and L-M reversed units (Figure 7).

L-M Unit
Make 4
M   L

L-M Reversed Unit
Make 4
L   M

Figure 7

8. Join two M pieces, two N pieces and one O piece with one each of the L-M and L-M reversed units to make row 4 for a Face block (Figure 8). Make four of row 4.

Row 4
Make 4
M   N   O

Figure 8

9. Again using the sew-and-flip technique, make four each of the P-Q and P-Q reversed units (Figure 9).

P-Q Unit
Make 4

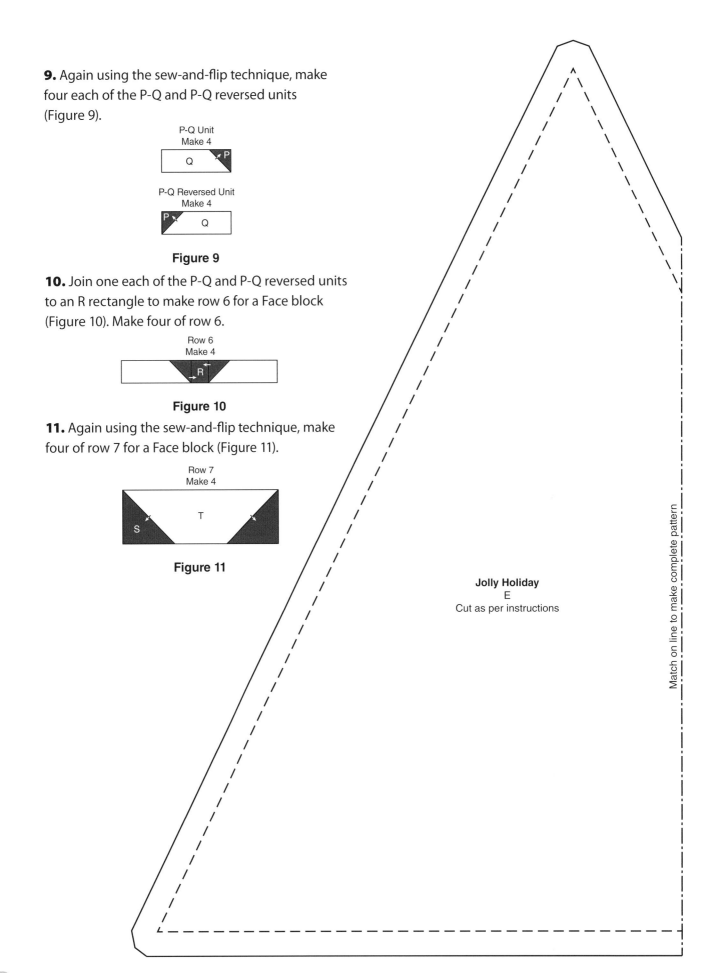

P-Q Reversed Unit
Make 4

Figure 9

10. Join one each of the P-Q and P-Q reversed units to an R rectangle to make row 6 for a Face block (Figure 10). Make four of row 6.

Row 6
Make 4

Figure 10

11. Again using the sew-and-flip technique, make four of row 7 for a Face block (Figure 11).

Row 7
Make 4

Figure 11

Jolly Holiday
E
Cut as per instructions

Match on line to make complete pattern

12. Join one each of rows 1–7 to complete a Face block (Figure 12). Make four Face blocks.

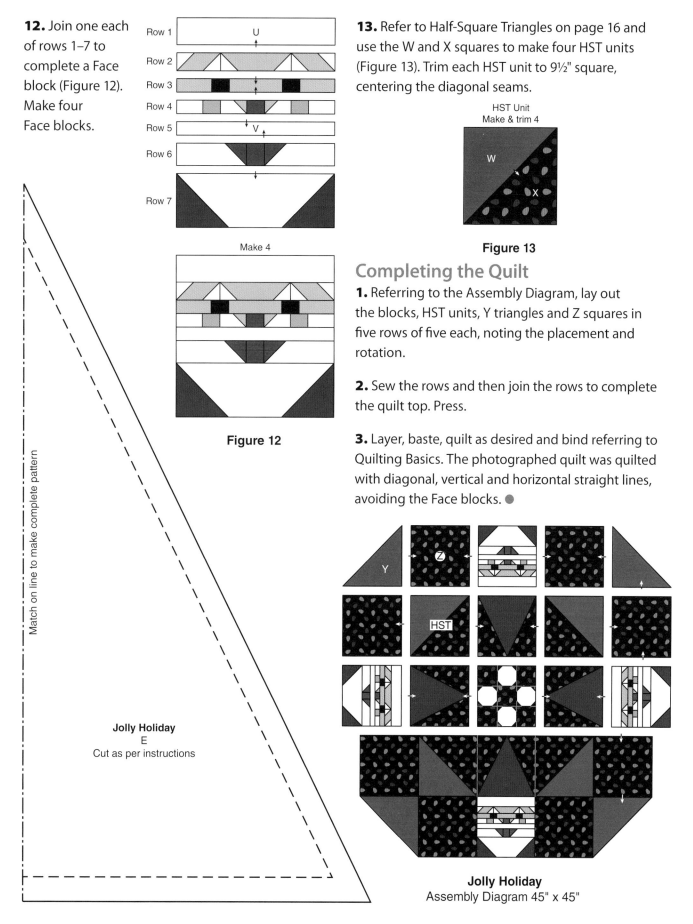

Row 1 — U

Row 2

Row 3

Row 4

Row 5 — V

Row 6

Row 7

Make 4

Figure 12

Match on line to make complete pattern

Jolly Holiday
E
Cut as per instructions

13. Refer to Half-Square Triangles on page 16 and use the W and X squares to make four HST units (Figure 13). Trim each HST unit to 9½" square, centering the diagonal seams.

HST Unit
Make & trim 4

W

X

Figure 13

Completing the Quilt

1. Referring to the Assembly Diagram, lay out the blocks, HST units, Y triangles and Z squares in five rows of five each, noting the placement and rotation.

2. Sew the rows and then join the rows to complete the quilt top. Press.

3. Layer, baste, quilt as desired and bind referring to Quilting Basics. The photographed quilt was quilted with diagonal, vertical and horizontal straight lines, avoiding the Face blocks. ●

Y

Z

HST

Jolly Holiday
Assembly Diagram 45" x 45"

Tumbling Gingerbread Table Runner

Create an inviting holiday table with these warm
and whimsical gingerbread men.

Designed & Quilted by Chris Malone

Skill Level
Beginner

Finished Size
Runner Size: 42" x 14"

Materials
- ⅓ yard white print
- ¼ yard tan tonal
- 1 (6") square red tonal
- 1 (10") square white tonal
- ¼ yard green print
- ⅜ yard red print
- 16" x 44" backing
- 16" x 44" batting*
- 10 (³⁄₁₆"-diameter) black buttons
- Paper-backed fusible web
- Basic sewing tools and supplies

*Warm & Natural cotton batting from The Warm Company used to
make sample.

Project Notes
Read all instructions before beginning this project.

Stitch right sides together using a ¼" seam
allowance unless otherwise specified.

Materials and cutting lists assume 40" of usable
fabric width for yardage.

Arrows indicate directions to press seams.

WOF – width of fabric
HST – half-square triangle ◻
QST – quarter-square triangle ◻

Cutting

From white print cut:
- 1 (10½" x 38½") A rectangle

From green print cut:
- 2 (2½" x 38½") B border strips
- 2 (2½" x 14½") C border strips

From red print cut:
- 4 (2½" x WOF) binding strips

Completing the Appliqué Panel
1. Refer to Raw-Edge Fusible Appliqué on page 26
and make the following appliqués.
- Tan tonal: five gingerbread boys
- Red tonal: five hearts
- White tonal: 10 arm trims; 10 leg trims

2. Center a gingerbread boy at each end of the
A rectangle, about 2" from the raw edges (Figure 1).
Place one gingerbread boy at the center, upside
down. Place the remaining two gingerbread boys
in the spaces between the others, at an angle as
if turning to do a cartwheel. Fuse in place and
machine blanket-stitch around the appliqués using
matching thread.

Figure 1

3. Referring to the photo, place a leg trim across each leg and an arm trim across each arm. Fuse in place. Place a heart on each gingerbread boy; fuse in place. Machine blanket-stitch around the appliqués using matching thread to complete the appliqué panel.

Completing the Runner

1. Referring to the Assembly Diagram, sew B strips to the long sides of the panel. Sew C strips to the short sides.

2. Referring to Quilting Basics, layer, baste and quilt as desired. The photographed runner was quilted with a candy cane design. Transfer the smile pattern to each face and quilt two times on the lines using black thread. Sew two buttons to each face for eyes.

3. Bind referring to Quilting Basics. ●

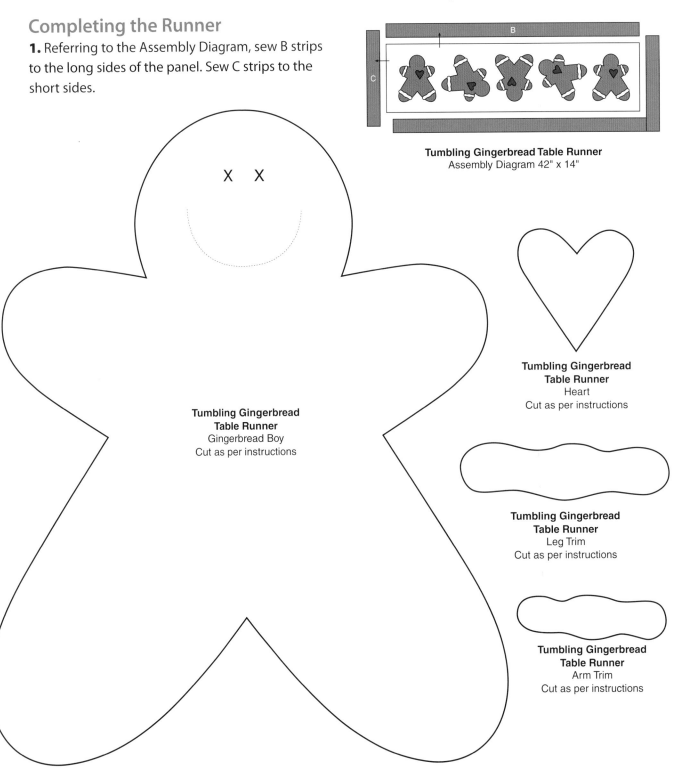

Tumbling Gingerbread Table Runner
Assembly Diagram 42" x 14"

Tumbling Gingerbread Table Runner
Gingerbread Boy
Cut as per instructions

Tumbling Gingerbread Table Runner
Heart
Cut as per instructions

Tumbling Gingerbread Table Runner
Leg Trim
Cut as per instructions

Tumbling Gingerbread Table Runner
Arm Trim
Cut as per instructions

Quilting Basics

The following is a reference guide. For more information, consult a comprehensive quilting book.

Quilt Backing & Batting

Cut your backing and batting 8" larger than the finished quilt-top size and 4" larger for quilts smaller than 50" square. *Note: Check with longarm quilter about their requirements, if applicable. For baby quilts not going to a longarm quilter 4"–6" overall may be sufficient.* If preparing the backing from standard-width fabrics, remove the selvages and sew two or three lengths together; press seams open. If using 108"-wide fabric, trim to size on the straight grain of the fabric. Prepare batting the same size as your backing.

Quilting

1. Press quilt top on both sides and trim all loose threads. *Note: If you are sending your quilt to a longarm quilter, contact them for specifics about preparing your quilt for quilting.*
2. Mark quilting design on quilt top. Make a quilt sandwich by layering the backing right side down, batting and quilt top centered right side up on flat surface and smooth out. Baste layers together using pins, thread basting or spray basting to hold. *Note: Tape or pin backing to surface to hold taut while layering and avoid puckers.*
3. Quilt as desired by hand or machine. Remove pins or basting as you quilt.
4. Trim batting and backing edges even with raw edges of quilt top.

Binding the Quilt

1. Join binding strips on short ends with diagonal seams to make one long strip; trim seams to ¼" and press seams open (Figure 1).

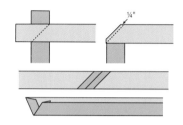

Figure 1

2. Fold ½" of one short end to wrong side and press. Fold the binding strip in half with wrong sides together along length, again referring to Figure 1; press.
3. Starting about 3" from the folded short end, sew binding to quilt top edges, matching raw edges and using a ¼" seam. Stop stitching ¼" from corner and backstitch (Figure 2).

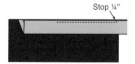

Stop ¼"

Figure 2

4. Fold binding up at a 45-degree angle to seam and then down even with quilt edges, forming a pleat at corner (Figure 3).

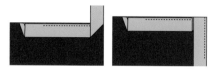

Figure 3

5. Resume stitching from corner edge as shown in Figure 3, down quilt side, backstitching ¼" from next corner. Repeat, mitering all corners, stitching to within 3" of starting point.
6. Trim binding, leaving enough length to tuck inside starting end and complete stitching (Figure 4).

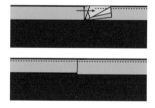

Figure 4

7. If stitching binding by hand, machine-sew binding to the front of the quilt and fold to the back before stitching. If stitching by machine, machine-sew binding to back of the quilt and fold to the front before stitching.

Special Thanks

Please join us in thanking the talented designers
whose work is featured in this collection.

Annette Falvo
Sunrise in Spring, 5

Michelle Freedman
Patchwork Heart Table Runner, 2

Joy Heimark
American Pride, 12

Roni Hickey
Blooming Pumpkins, 22

Andy Knowlton
Fireworks & Stars, 17

Cathey Laird
Jolly Holiday, 38

Chris Malone
Tumbling Gingerbread
Table Runner, 44

Jill Metzger
Sasha Mae, 27

Wendy Sheppard
In a Row, 9
Pumpkin Boo!, 31
Tree Farm, 35

Supplies

We would like to thank the following manufacturers who provided
materials to our designers to make sample projects for this book.

Patchwork Heart Table Runner, page 2: Fabrics from the
Shadow Play collection from Maywood Studio.

Sunrise in Spring, page 5: Fabrics from the Happy Hearts and
Shadow Blush collections from Benartex.

In a Row, page 9: Fabrics from the 30s Playtime collection by
Chloe's Closet for Moda Fabrics; 50 wt. Mako thread from
Aurifil; Tuscany silk batting from Hobbs Bonded Fibers.

Pumpkin Boo!, page 31: Fabrics from the Awesome Autumn
collection by Sandy Gervais and the Bee Cross Stitch
collection by Lori Holt for Riley Blake Designs; Tuscan silk
batting from Hobbs Bonded Fibers; 50 wt. Mako thread from
Aurifil.

Tree Farm, page 35: Fabrics from the A Christmas Carol
collection by 3 Sisters for Moda Fabrics; Tuscany silk batting
from Hobbs Bonded Fibers; 50 wt. Mako thread from Aurifil.

Jolly Holiday, page 38: Fabrics from the Jolly Holiday collection
by Patrick Lose for Northcott; Warm & Natural cotton batting
from The Warm Company; 50 wt. Mako thread from Aurifil.

Tumbling Gingerbread Table Runner, page 44: Warm &
Natural cotton batting from The Warm Company.

 Published by Annie's, 306 East Parr Road, Berne, IN 46711. Printed in USA. Copyright © 2024 Annie's. All rights reserved. This publication
may not be reproduced in part or in whole without written permission from the publisher.

RETAIL STORES: If you would like to carry this publication or any other Annie's publications, visit AnniesWSL.com.

Every effort has been made to ensure that the instructions in this publication are complete and accurate. We cannot, however, take responsibility for human error,
typographical mistakes or variations in individual work. Please visit AnniesCustomerService.com to check for pattern updates.

ISBN:

979-8-89253-305-8

2 3 4 5 6 7 8 9